DIESELS on the REGIONS

SOUTHERN REGION

Plate 1: For many years, the staple motive power for the Southern Region has been a fleet of Birmingham RC&W Type 3 Class 33 locomotives. The fleet, currently standing at 94, is allocated to Eastleigh and Hither Green depots. Here, Eastleigh-allocated No. 33026 passes Pirbright Junction, on 15th April 1980, with the 12.28 Exeter to Waterloo train.

Colin Marsden

Plate 2: From the early 1980s, the Southern's main line between Waterloo and Exeter, hitherto operated by Class 33 locomotives, has been in the capable hands of Western Region-allocated Class 50 engines. In this view, No. 50038 *Formidable* hurries the 11.10 Waterloo to Exeter train past Hampton Court Junction, to the west of Surbiton, on 28th March 1981.

Colin Marsden

DIESELS on the REGIONS

SOUTHERN REGION

Colin J. Marsden

Oxford Publishing Company

INTRODUCTION

Of the five BR regions, the Southern is the smallest in terms of area but comes fourth in route mileage, with the Scottish coming last. However, with the Southern Region being predominantly electric orientated with only 94 main line diesel-electric, 47 shunting and 47 electro-diesel locomotives in its allocation, locomotive-hauled movements are at somewhat of a premium. From these basic statistics it would seem that the Southern Region does not have much to offer the locomotive enthusiast, but how wrong this assumption would be, and it is hoped that this 96 page volume will indicate the variety of locomotive-hauled trains that operate on the region.

The story of diesel traction on Southern metals dates back nearly fifty years to 1936, when the Southern Railway took delivery of three English Electric-powered shunting locomotives, in an experiment to replace steam traction from some marshalling yards. Around the period of nationalization (1948) the Southern Railway, in company with the LMS, was involved in trials with main line diesel-electric locomotives, which proved to be very reliable and satisfactory, and this paved the way for the modern railway scene that we see today. In fact, it is only an updated and uprated version of the same series of diesel engine, that powered the SR prototype locomotives, that powers the Class 50 engines of today. The first real step forward in the demise of steam traction from the main lines came following the modernization plans of 1955, when it was decided to dieselize the London to Hastings route using diesel electric multiple unit stock. This eventually led to the placing of orders for nearly 100 main line Type 3 (now Class 33) locomotives from Birmingham RC&W Ltd. for main line passenger and freight duties. Further steps to oust steam came during the early 1960s when the first of six prototype electro-diesel locomotives was built at Eastleigh, and orders for a further 43 locomotives were placed with English Electric during 1966/7.

Today, the Southern Region not only uses its own fleets of main line locomotives but has diagrams for many machines from other regions, including Western Region Class 50 locomotives that operate the Waterloo to Exeter service and numerous Class 47 locomotives, none of which are actually allocated to the Southern Region but are used for inter-regional services.

This book does not set out to portray every class of diesel that has seen operation on the Southern Region, but it is hoped will give a broad outline of motive power on a wide variety of routes and duties.

In common with other volumes in the series, *Diesels on the Regions*, this book has been divided into various sections, the main ones being headed by a map giving an indication of the area covered in that particular section. Where possible, sub-headings have been given, grouping together photographs of a similar type or of operations over a similar part of the network or section.

I would like to thank the many modern traction photographers who have assisted with providing material for this project, and also to record my appreciation of the complete freedom in choice of material used and the design accorded to me by the Publishers.

Colin J. Marsden
Surbiton
May 1984

Copyright © 1984 Oxford Publishing Co. & C. J. Marsden.

ISBN 0-86093-243-5

Typesetting by:
Aquarius Typesetting Services, New Milton, Hants.

Printed in Great Britain by:
Biddles Ltd., Guildford, Surrey.

Published by:
Oxford Publishing Co.
Link House
West Street
POOLE, Dorset

THE LONDON AREA

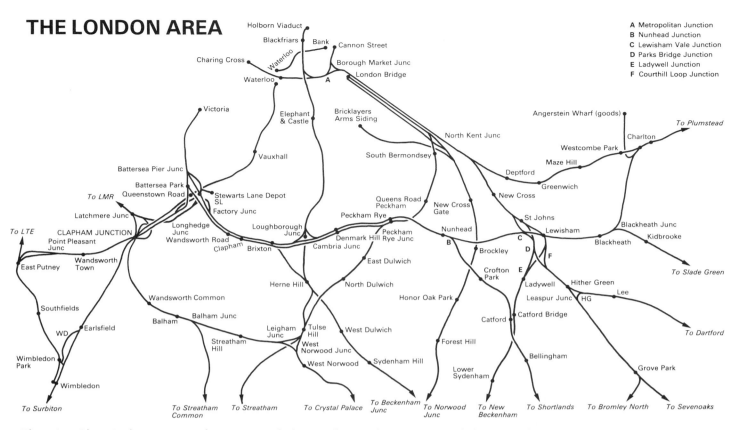

A Metropolitan Junction
B Nunhead Junction
C Lewisham Vale Junction
D Parks Bridge Junction
E Ladywell Junction
F Courthill Loop Junction

Plate 3: Class 33 locomotives have certainly been allocated some unusual duties in their careers, but probably one of the most memorable in the life of No. 33113 was on 16th November 1982, when it hauled new generation Class 455 electric multiple unit No. 455805 to Waterloo from Strawberry Hill for a press inspection. The locomotive is seen here positioning the unit in platform 15 at Waterloo.

Colin Marsden

WESTERN SECTION

Plate 4 (above): Although Class 50 locomotives took over the majority of Waterloo to Exeter services from 1980, the 01.45 Waterloo to Yeovil passenger/newspaper service is still Class 33 powered. When this photograph was taken, on 22nd April 1981, the train was awaiting departure headed by No. 33020.

Colin Marsden

Plate 5 (left): Night photography at London stations is not as difficult as it sounds, with modern high-powered station lighting giving a good even illumination of the subject. With headlight and roof-mounted marker lights glowing, Class 50 No. 50019 *Ramillies* heads the 19.10 Exeter service on 20th October 1980.

Colin Marsden

LSWR MAIN LINE

Plate 6 (above): Departures from the 21 platforms at Waterloo filter into only eight actual running lines within a quarter mile of the buffer stops. Winding its way from platform 14 to the 'down' main through line, on 23rd October 1979, Class 33 No. 33029 departs with the 13.00 West of England service just prior to the introduction of the more powerful Class 50 locomotives.

Colin Marsden

Plate 7 (left): Class 50 locomotives had a somewhat marked record of failures when they first took over the Southern route to the west, but following the refurbishing scheme, some creditable performances have been recorded. However, on 10th August 1981, No. 50020 *Revenge*, with the 09.40 Exeter to Waterloo service, failed at Surbiton and was rescued by sister locomotive No. 50036 *Victorious*. The combination is seen here between Vauxhall and Waterloo.

Colin Marsden

Plate 8 (left): The SR electric multiple unit fleet is normally able to operate in the most extreme weather conditions, but prolonged heavy snow and icy conditions during the second week of January 1982 caused havoc to services, and numerous electric multiple units had to be assisted by locomotives. Class 33 No. 33021 is seen approaching West London Junction hauling Class 423 (4VEP) stock with a Portsmouth working on 9th January.

Colin Marsden

AROUND WIMBLEDON

Plate 11 (above): On a bright 18th August 1980, a Class 50 locomotive, No. 50026 *Indomitable*, in original condition, passes the staff halt adjacent to Wimbledon Park electric multiple unit depot, while in charge of the 07.37 Exeter to Waterloo train. Seen on the left is the Wimbledon Flyover, carrying the 'up' local line, and it is from this point to the capital that the two local tracks run adjacent, reducing awkward and conflicting moves nearer to Waterloo.

Colin Marsden

Plate 12 (below): In the closing years of the 1970s, new purpose-built electric multiple unit accommodation was built adjacent to Wimbledon Park Depot. The new depot, named Wimbledon East, is seen here as Class 50 No. 50011 *Centurion* passes with the 11.10 departure from Waterloo. The depot has accommodation for some 250 electric multiple unit cars.

Colin Marsden

Plate 9 (above left): Over the years, the Clapham Cutting area, between Clapham Junction and Earlsfield, has been a regular haunt for railway photographers, and today much patience is required if they aim to capture anything other than one of the endless procession of electric multiple units. Formed of a Western Region Class 117 three car unit, the 11.54 (SO) Waterloo to Basingstoke train was observed, on 7th August 1965, near Earlsfield.

John Scrace

Plate 10 (left): Storming away from the 40m.p.h. speed restriction on the 'down' fast line through Clapham Junction, Class 50 No. 50016 *Barham* heads a rake of Western Region Mk. II vehicles on the 11.10 Waterloo to Exeter service of 17th April 1981. The gradient climbs at a steady 1 in 338 towards the south-west from Clapham Junction, which requires the locomotive to be under full power.

Colin Marsden

Plate 13 (above): Wimbledon Station is seven miles seventeen chains from Waterloo, and has a start to pass time (for locomotive-hauled trains) of eleven minutes. Swinging around the comparatively tight curve at the London end of the station, on 25th August 1980, is Class 50 No. 50024 *Vanguard* with the 17.00 Waterloo to Exeter train.

Colin Marsden

Plate 14 (below): The London area lines of the South-Western Division see comparatively little freight traffic, except for around Clapham Junction. Wimbledon, however, has a small yard to the west of the station which handles traffic for the nearby signal department workshops. Having crossed from the West yard to the 'up' through line, on 1st April 1982, Class 33 No. 33035 hauls a short-fitted freight through Wimbledon Station, and is bound for Clapham Junction.

Colin Marsden

WINDSOR LINES

Plate 15 (above): The lines radiating from Clapham Junction towards Barnes, Twickenham and Hounslow are referred to in operating circles as the Windsor lines, and are hosts to a sizeable amount of inter-regional and inter-divisional freight traffic. Class 33 No. 33039 hauls a heavy Murphy aggregate train towards Clapham Junction from the Eastern Region.

Colin Marsden

Plate 16 (right): The section of line as far as Barnes is four tracked, from where two track sections continue to Richmond and Hounslow. The Allington to Westbury empty stone train, headed by Class 33 locomotives Nos. 33037 and 33049, slows down for a signal check at Barnes, on 27th October 1982, before taking the Hounslow loop line to Staines, Woking, Basingstoke and the Western Region.

Colin Marsden

CENTRAL SECTION

Plate 17 (right): Of the three Southern Divisions, Central sees the least amount of locomotive-hauled traffic with movements into Victoria (Central Division) being rare. However, when transporting Heads of State and world dignitaries on State Visits to this country, after their arrival at Gatwick and conveyance by the Royal Train, locomotive-hauled trains visit the station. On 13th February 1967 the Soviet Prime Minister, Mr Kosygin, at the end of a State Visit, was transported by train to Gatwick. Class JB No. E6036 stands at Victoria, prior to departure, carrying a special Anglo-Russian headboard.

Author's Collection

AROUND VICTORIA

Plate 18 (below): Although officially traversing South-Eastern Division tracks approaching Victoria, this illustration has been included in this section for reasons of continuity. For many years, the highlight of the day was the arrival at Victoria of the 'Night Ferry' from Paris. The train was usually formed of Continental stock and powered by a Class 73 locomotive. On 16th July 1979 it was the turn of No. 73119 to perform the honours.

Brian Morrison

STEWARTS LANE

Plate 19 (above): Home for the region's fleet of Class 73 electro-diesel locomotives is Stewarts Lane Depot, at Battersea, situated just outside Victoria Station. The depot is also responsible for the maintenance of a large number of electric multiple unit trains and wagons. Photographed when new in 1967, Class JB No. E6039 shunts a formation of TC stock in the depot yard.

GEC Traction Ltd.

Plate 20 (right): One of the most useful cross-London connections joins all three divisions between Factory Junction, near Brixton, and Clapham Junction. Approaching Longhedge Junction from Factory Junction on 24th September 1980, Class 47 No. 47049 hauls the 08.27 Allington to Westbury empty roadstone train, formed completely of privately-owned hoppers.

Colin Marsden

INTER-REGIONAL FREIGHT

Plate 21 (above): The largest source of locomotive-hauled traffic in the London area of the Central Division is the cross-London freight traffic which has, for many years, brought a variety of motive power to the otherwise electric multiple unit world. On 19th November 1979, passing through the Central Division's Clapham Cutting, Class 37 No. 37130 provides the power for a Temple Mills (Eastern Region) to Norwood freight.

Colin Marsden

Plate 22 (below): In the days of four character headcodes, inter-regional services to the Southern Region were identified by a letter 'O' as the second character. In this view, taken on 15th August 1973, Class 25 No. D7526 departs from Clapham Junction and heads towards Wandsworth Common, hauling the daily class 7 freight working from Willesden to Norwood.

Brian Morrison

Plate 23 (above right): Many railway enthusiasts are aware of the daily Acton to Norwood freight service which, for a number of years, was powered by the now extinct Class 52 'Western' locomotives. During the 1977-81 period, the train was often to be seen powered by Class 50 locomotives, giving a rare chance to observe one of these powerful Type 4 engines hauling a freight train off the Western Region. No. 50007 *Hercules* is seen, on 25th November 1980, passing Streatham Hill.

Colin Marsden

Plate 24 (right): Today, the Acton to Norwood freight is usually hauled by a Class 47, and is possibly a less interesting engine to photograph. With a comparatively light fully-fitted train in tow, No. 47060 passes the wet platforms of Streatham Hill Station on 1st April 1982. In the 'down' direction the train operates via Streatham Hill and Gipsy Hill, and returns 'up' via Thornton Heath and Streatham Common.

Colin Marsden

Plate 25 (left): London's south-eastern approaches see few locomotive-hauled trains, although some of the main line services are diesel-powered by means of diesel multiple units, and are therefore, eligible for inclusion here. The first step to oust steam trains on the Hastings line was in 1957, when the new Cannon Street/ Charing Cross to Hastings diesel multiple unit service was inaugurated. Pictured here, on 6th May 1957, is the 17.18 Hastings service departing from Cannon Street, formed of 6S units Nos. 1003 and 1004.
Brian Morrison

Plate 26 (below left): Currently, an hourly service operates between London and Hastings, with additional services during the peak periods. Three types of unit operate these services, including Class 201 (6S), Class 202 (6L) and Class 203 (5L). Departing from Waterloo East on 13th September 1982, 5L No. 1035 forms the 13.45 Charing Cross to Hastings service.
Brian Morrison

Plate 28 (below): It is many years since regular locomotive-hauled passenger services operated in the London area of the South Eastern Division but, however, prior to the Kent Coast electrification being fully implemented, and after the demise of steam from some routes, diesel-hauled services were instigated. On 3rd June 1961, Birmingham RC&W Type 3 locomotive, No. D6549 passes St. Johns with the 08.52 (SO) Charing Cross to Deal holiday train.
John Scrace

Plate 27 (above): The many thousands of daily commuters who use London Bridge Station would be rather surprised to see this train parked in the platform during the average working day. In connection with nearby engineering work, Class 73 No. 73139 stands in the platform, on 10th February 1980, attached to a permanent way crane.
Andrew French

HITHER GREEN

Plate 29 (above): In south-east London, the area around Hither Green is frequented by many railway enthusiasts, mainly due to the depot being adjacent to the station, the large number of locomotive-hauled freight trains and the occasional excursion passenger trains that pass through. Class 47 No. 47532 passes the station, on 9th October 1982, with a special from the Midland Region, bound for one of the south-eastern holiday resorts.

Brian Morrison

Plate 30 (left): The traction maintenance depot at Hither Green is responsible for thirty seven of the region's Class 33 locomotives, in addition to carrying out sundry repairs to visiting Class 08, 09 and 73 locomotives. Resplendent after a recent visit to the BREL works at Eastleigh, Class 33 No. 33034 stands inside the shed on 9th October 1982.

Colin Marsden

Plate 31 (above): On the evening of 5th November 1967 Hither Green hit world headlines, when the 19.53 Hastings to Charing Cross train was derailed to the south of the station by a broken rail. The train, formed of a twelve car formation of Hastings diesel multiple unit stock, was completely derailed except for the leading vehicle, and many carriages overturned, thus resulting in the tragic loss of 49 lives, with a further 78 seriously injured. This illustration shows the derailment scene on the following day, after the first two vehicles had been removed.

British Railways

Plate 32 (right): At Hither Green, the start of the elimination of steam traction came during the mid-1950s when some of the SR/BR 0-6-0 diesel shunters, which were built at Ashford, were allocated to the depot. Replacements for main line power did not arrive until 1959 when the first Birmingham RC&W Type 3, No. D6500 was delivered. An 0-6-0 shunter, No. 15221 is seen here during 1953 painted in black livery and being fuelled.

GEC Traction Ltd.

CLAPHAM JUNCTION

Plate 33 (left): Trains on both the South Western and Central Divisions can be seen, together with numerous cross-London services, at the most famous junction in the world, Clapham. A large 53 road shunting yard is also provided. Approaching the station and slowing down for the 40m.p.h. speed restriction, Class 33 No. 33004 heads the 11.10 West of England service on 5th March 1981.

Colin Marsden

Plate 34 (below): Branch line services are not a thing many people would expect to find operating from Clapham Junction but, however, two trains operate daily each way between Clapham Junction and Kensington Olympia, primarily to convey GPO staff to offices adjacent to Kensington Olympia Station. For many years, the morning service was operated by a Class 33 locomotive and two coaches, while the afternoon train was formed of a Class 33 and TC stock. However, from late 1982, the morning service has been operated by a Western Region diesel multiple unit. In this scene, Class 33/2 No. 33210 awaits departure from Clapham Junction with the 08.45 service to Kensington on 11th August 1981.

Colin Marsden

Plate 35 (right): Two Class 08 or 09 locomotives allocated to Selhurst (SU) are normally to be found on shunting duties in Clapham Junction yard, which is responsible for all locomotive-hauled services from Waterloo, various van and departmental trains, as well as the servicing of electric multiple unit stock during the day. Class 09, No. 09012 is seen shunting a rake of Mk. I stock on 5th March 1981.

Colin Marsden

Plate 36 (below): One of the landmarks of Clapham Junction is the massive gantry-mounted Clapham Junction 'A' signal box. From the war until May 1965, a special steel-plated roof was provided but unfortunately, in 1965, the box sagged under pressure of weight, and following repairs the plated roof was removed. Passing under this interesting structure, and heading an unfitted coal train to the London Midland Region from Gravesend, during the summer of 1974, is Class 45 'Peak' No. 36.

Brian Morrison

Plate 37 (above): Freight trains in abundance can be observed on the Central Division side at Clapham Junction, from where they descend and pass under the Central and South Western main lines and head for Latchmere Junction, going from there to the Western, London Midland or Eastern Regions. The train illustrated here is passing Clapham Junction Station headed by a Class 52 'Western', No. D1040 *Western Queen*, and is the daily Acton to Norwood freight.

John Faulkner

Plate 38 (left): Passenger trains from Victoria to East Grinstead and Uckfield take the form of diesel electric multiple unit stock, usually of Class 205 (3H) or Class 207 (3D). In this 1981 summer view of the Central Division main line platforms, two Class 207 units pass while operating Victoria to Uckfield services. The black diamond on the front of the stock indicates that the guard's van and traction equipment is at that end of the unit.

Colin Marsden

Plate 39 (right): Although the tracks of the South Western and Central Divisions meet up at Clapham Junction, and indeed run parallel for a mile, there is no physical connection between them, although one installed during the 1960s was soon removed on economic grounds. The 17.00 Waterloo to Exeter train, powered by refurbished Class 50 No. 50036 *Victorious*, heads for Clapham Cutting on 12th August 1981, while a Class 508 traverses the 'up' local line.

Colin Marsden

Plate 40 (below): In recent years, passenger returns have been such that a through service from Brighton to Manchester has been operating, bringing regular Class 47-hauled trains to the Central Division main line. In this view, No. 47088 *Samson* is about to be overtaken by Class 420 (4BIG) No. 7042 while operating the 15.00 Brighton to Manchester service on 12th August 1981, and slowing down to take the spur to the West London line at Clapham Junction.

Colin Marsden

SOUTH WESTERN DIVISION

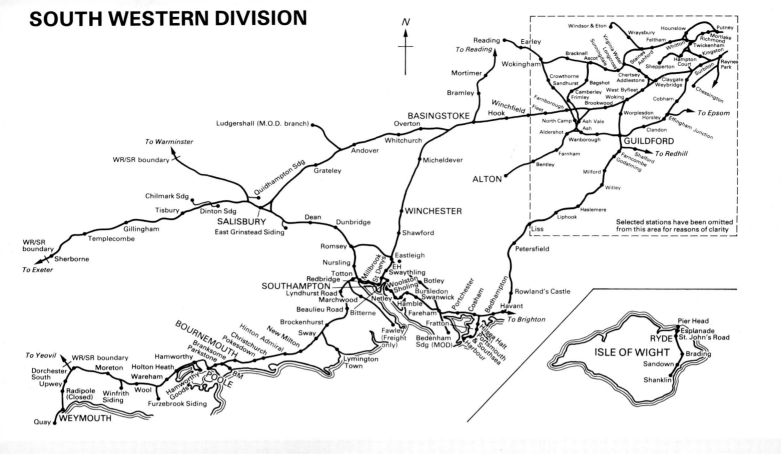

MAIN LINES

Plate 41: The South-Western main line commenced the gradual change from steam to diesel during the mid-1960s, following the delivery of Birmingham RC&W Type 3 locomotives to Eastleigh. The Bournemouth line was one of the first to sample Type 3 power and, on 19th June 1965, a Bournemouth to Waterloo train is seen approaching Raynes Park led by No. D6549.

A. Swain

Plate 42 (above): Although today Eastleigh has an allocation of fifty seven Class 33 locomotives, very few operate main line passenger duties. However, the boat trains to and from Southampton Docks are occasionally operated by this class of locomotive. In this scene, push-pull fitted No. 33106 passes New Malden with empty coaches bound for Clapham Junction, after forming a school special to Southampton Docks on 14th April 1980.

Colin Marsden

Plate 43 (below): During a heavy snowfall, Class 33 No. 33010 pulls a twelve car formation of Class 423 (4VEP) electric multiple unit stock away from Surbiton early in January 1982. If this Class 33 had been one of the nineteen push-pull fitted examples, it could have operated in multiple with the electric multiple units giving an additional 3,000hp, although in conditions like these, it is unlikely that the pick-up shoes would have made good contact with the live rail.

Colin Marsden

THROUGH SUBURBIA

Plate 44 (left): The ten super or big electro-diesels of Class 74 were a unique breed, being converted in 1967 from the straight 2,500hp electric locomotives of Class 71. The Class 74s usually operated on the Waterloo to Bournemouth line, and one of their regular duties was hauling the Waterloo to Weymouth boat trains as far as Bournemouth. No. 74005 is seen passing Surbiton, during 1977, with the 09.54 service from Waterloo.

Colin Marsden

Plate 45 (left): When steam still reigned supreme on the Waterloo to West of England route during the 1950s, three SR and two LMS prototype English Electric-powered locomotives operated various services, mainly to gauge their operating potential for the future. In this view, SR No. 10202 passes Surbiton on 3rd August 1952 with the 07.00 Yeovil to Waterloo service.

John Faulkner

Plate 46 (below): It was not until 1972 that the Waterloo to Exeter route became the stamping ground for Class 33 locomotives as, from the demise of steam, the Class 42 'Warship' engines operated the service. Although Class 33s could not match the performance of the former power, some creditable operating was given by these Type 3 locomotives. No. 33022 is seen passing Hampton Court Junction, on 4th April 1980, with the 11.00 Waterloo to Exeter service.

Colin Marsden

Plate 47:   Class 33 locomotives have a top speed of 85m.p.h. and on most occasions this maximum is recorded for at least part of the run, usually between Waterloo and Salisbury. No. 33017 passes Weybridge at the head of the 10.10 Waterloo to Salisbury service on 28th March 1981, and in the background, standing in the station, can be seen the branch train bound for Staines.

Colin Marsden

WOKING AREA

Plate 48 (above left): The Waterloo to Exeter line currently has a two hourly service, with trains leaving Waterloo at the intermediate hour bound for Salisbury only. With snowploughs fitted, No. 33033 pulls away from the Woking stop and accelerates towards West Byfleet with an early morning Exeter to Waterloo train on 5th February 1981.

Colin Marsden

Plate 49 (left): A train that brings interesting motive power to the South Western Division main line is the three times weekly 04.20 Ripple Lane to Micheldever and the 09.17 return service. This train can be operated by Class 31, 37 or 47 locomotives and Class 37 No. 37041 is seen here, on 17th August 1982, between Woking and West Byfleet, with empty tanks returning to the Eastern Region.

Colin Marsden

Plate 50 (above): The first stop for the Waterloo to West of England services is Woking, 25 miles from Waterloo and, in the current timetable, locomotive-hauled services are scheduled to arrive at Woking within 26 minutes of departure from Waterloo. One of the earliest photographs of a diesel operating the West of England service, was on 15th October 1951 when SR prototype No. 10202 powered the 11.00 service from Waterloo, seen here departing from Woking.

Author's Collection

Plate 51 (right): To the west of Woking Station are sizeable yards on both the east and west sides of the line. These yards are mainly used for the formation of ballast trains and weekend permanent way specials and, in addition, a handful of van trains are dealt with daily. This photograph shows Class 09, No. 09002 shunting GUV and CCT vans in Woking 'down' yard on 15th May 1981.

Colin Marsden

Plate 52 (above): The stock which operates the nightly Waterloo to Bournemouth passenger/newspaper services returns empty, during the following morning, to Clapham Junction, and it is often convenient to use this as a test train for locomotives that have been repaired at Eastleigh Works. On 15th May 1981, Class 33/2 No. 33205 provided the power.

Colin Marsden

Plate 53 (left): Stone trains formed of privately-owned hopper wagons make regular trips on the South Western Division main line when originating from or returning to Westbury, usually operating to motorway construction sites or aggregate stone terminals. On 9th April 1981, Class 47 No. 47110 passes Woking Junction with empty hoppers belonging to the Amalgamated Roadstone Co., returning to Westbury from Angerstein Wharf.

Colin Marsden

Plate 54 (above): To the west of Woking, the South Western Division main line passes through the deep tree-lined St. Johns Cutting, and it is at this point that 'up' trains start to decelerate for the Woking Station stop. With power shut off and the brakes starting to rub, Class 50 No. 50015 *Valiant* makes an easy approach to Woking with the 09.38 Exeter to Waterloo working during the spring of 1982.

Colin Marsden

Plate 55 (right): To the West of Brookwood lies Pirbright Junction, where the Alton branch diverges. This section of line usually sees only locomotive-hauled trains to Farnham ballast tip, although on 1st October 1982 the line was host to the Royal Train conveying HRH The Prince of Wales on a special visit to Aldershot. Here the returning stock from the Royal Special, headed by Class 33 No. 33027 *Earl Mountbatten of Burma*, forming the 10.18 working from Aldershot to Wolverton Works, approaches Foxhills Tunnel, near Pirbright Junction.

Andrew French

Plate 56: Although the booked motive power for Waterloo to Exeter services is now Class 50, it is not uncommon for Class 33 or 47 locomotives to be substituted due to failure or other technical difficulties. On 15th April 1981, the 15.00 Waterloo to Exeter train is seen near Pirbright Junction, with Class 33 No. 33002 providing the power.

Colin Marsden

INTO HAMPSHIRE

Plate 57 (above): One source of freight traffic to British Rail is the Ford Motor Co., who have large premises near Eastleigh. Trains formed of their products, in this case Transit vans, are regularly transported by rail to the north. On 9th April 1981, Class 47 No. 47035 is seen at Bramshot, between Fleet and Farnborough, hauling twenty one carflats conveying some 63 Ford Transit vans.

Colin Marsden

Plate 58 (right): The Southern Region's South Western Division main line to the west was, for many years, the envy of rival railway companies because of its highly commendable track, although, in recent years, the general condition has been in decline and many speed restrictions are now imposed. On 15th April 1980, passing some 'wet' patches on the 'down' line, Class 33 locomotive No. 33017 is seen at Newnham, near Basingstoke, with the 06.50 service from Yeovil to Waterloo.

Colin Marsden

Plate 59 (above):   It seems strange, today, to think that the South Western Division main line to the west of Pirbright Junction was not electrified until 1966/7, meaning that all services west thereof had to be steam or, latterly, diesel-operated. On 30th May 1954, the 11.00 westbound 'Atlantic Coast Express' (ACE), Waterloo to Torrington/Padstow service, passes near Fleet headed by SR diesel No. 10203.

British Railways

Plate 60 (below):   With nineteen 45 ton GLW two axle tank wagons in tow, Class 37 No. 37021 traverses the 'up' slow line near Winchfield, on 15th April 1982, with the 09.17 Micheldever to Ripple Lane train. On the four track sections of the Southern Region, it is usual practice for freight traffic to use the slow lines, but when on two track sections, freight traffic has to be carefully 'slotted in' to ensure passenger trains are not unduly delayed.

Andrew French

Plate 61 (above): The Southern is the only region to operate dual-powered locomotives, these being those that can either generate their own power by a diesel engine or collect power from an outside source, the third rail. The idea was first placed on the drawing boards of the Southern in the late 1940s, but it was not until 1961 that the first locomotive was built. Painted in immaculate green livery with a small yellow warning panel, the prototype electro-diesel No. E6001 approaches Basingstoke while returning to Eastleigh Works after its maiden test run to Woking during August 1961.

Author's Collection

Plate 62 (right): A proven useful link line to the Southern Region is the one between Basingstoke and Reading. This line is operated by the Southern Region as far as Southcote Junction, to the west of Reading West Station, and the inter-regional passenger and freight services from the south-west to the north traverse this route. On 5th June 1980, Class 33/1 No. 33114 pulls away from Basingstoke with the 11.35 Poole to Newcastle train and heads towards Bramley.

Andrew French

Plate 63 (left): Two large Freightliner terminals are situated on the Southern Region in the Southampton area, and both are served by several Class 4 Freightliner trains each day, most having traversed the Basingstoke to Reading line. With only a few empty spaces on its train of container flats, Class 47 No. 47290 approaches Basingstoke, on 9th April 1979, with a southbound Freightliner train.

Andrew French

Plate 64 (below): There are two passenger stations on the Basingstoke to Reading line, situated at Bramley and Mortimer, that fall into Southern Region operating territory. These stations are served by an hourly d.m.u. service between Portsmouth, Basingstoke and Reading while inter-regional express passenger and freight traffic is slotted between these services. Push-pull fitted Class 33/1 locomotive No. 33108 passes Minchens Bridge, near Bramley, with a Fawley bound oil train from the London Midland Region on 18th October 1979.

Andrew French

READING - BASINGSTOKE

Plate 65 (above): Inter-regional passenger services from the Midlands and the north to the south-east are now operated by e.t.h.-fitted Class 47/4 locomotives. After departing from Reading, most of these through services call at Basingstoke, Winchester, Southampton, and Bournemouth on the way to their destination of either Poole or Weymouth. The 07.20 Liverpool to Poole train slows down for the Winchester stop as it passes the Baltic siding on 7th July 1981.

Colin Marsden

TOWARDS WINCHESTER

Plate 66 (right): Winchester has a population of over 32,000 and is therefore served by both semi-fast and stopping services from Bournemouth to Waterloo, in addition to a number of inter-regional services. However, one service that did not stop at Winchester during the 1981/2 timetable was the 09.55 Weymouth to Leeds, seen here storming through the station on 7th July 1981 with Class 47 No. 47097 providing the power.

Colin Marsden

EASTLEIGH - BOURNEMOUTH

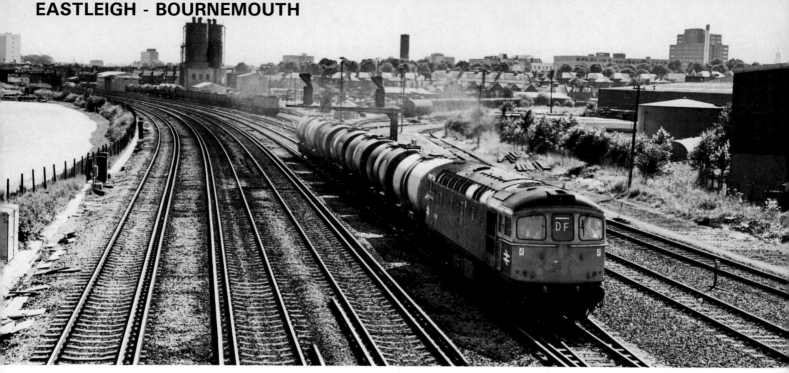

Plate 67 (above): Fawley Oil Refinery on Southampton Water has for many years provided the railway with a considerable amount of revenue, with oil trains departing to most parts of the country. Passing Bevois Park yard, between Eastleigh and Southampton, Class 33 No. 33061 heads an afternoon Fawley to London Midland Region oil train, formed of 45 ton GLW tanks.

Colin Marsden

Plate 71 (right): The summer only Waterloo to Weymouth Quay boat train service for the Channel Islands is operated by a Class 73 electro-diesel between Waterloo and Bournemouth, but as the journey on to Weymouth would be too taxing for the locomotive's 600hp diesel engine, a Class 33 diesel operates the train from Bournemouth. To convey passengers to London off the overnight sailing from the Channel Islands, a train departs from the quay at 06.45 headed by a Class 33 which in turn is replaced at Bournemouth with a Class 73. Here, on 12th August 1982, Class 73 No. 73113 waits to relieve Class 33 No. 33109.

Michael Collins

Plate 68 (above): For many years during the 1970s and early 1980s, Class 33 locomotives operated on a number of inter-regional services, usually to and from Reading. Standing at Southampton on 25th September 1980, Class 33/1 No. 33116 leads the 11.35 Poole to Newcastle working, for which the locomotive should be displaying headcode 92 (as far as Basingstoke) but for some reason, the driver considered that two white blanks were sufficient.

Colin Marsden

Plate 69 (right): The section of line between Southampton and Bournemouth offers the railway photographer some very pleasant scenery. Class 47 No. 47032, immediately identifiable by having the double arrow logo beneath the driver's assistant's window, passes near Hinton Admiral with the 14.55 Bournemouth to Liverpool service. The Class 47 locomotive will operate this train to Reading, where it will be replaced by another of the same class taking it on to Birmingham where a 25kV a.c. electric locomotive will complete the journey to Liverpool.

Colin Marsden

Plate 70: With empty coaching stock bound for Clapham Junction yard, Class 33/1 No. 33107 applies full power to lift its load of some 350 tons up the 1 in 103 gradient away from Hinton Admiral and past the village of Walkford, on 13th April 1982. The stock had operated to the west with a special train from Waterloo to Poole earlier in the day.

Colin Marsden

Plate 72 (above): Bournemouth, until 6th September 1965, had two stations; Central and West. However, with the modernization of the main line taking effect, and the demise of steam traction only some eighteen months away, all services were transferred to Central Station. No. D6536, a Birmingham RC&W Type 3, stands at Bournemouth West on Good Friday, in 1964, while in the background, the 'Bournemouth Belle' Pullman stock can be seen.

Colin Caddy

Plate 73 (left): When the South Western Division main line was electrified in 1967, it was thought uneconomic to electrify the section west of Bournemouth and, therefore, all trains for Weymouth had still to be locomotive-operated. The normal passenger service is worked by Class 33/1 locomotives hauling or propelling Class 491 (TC) stock. On 11th August 1982, No. 33116 provides the power for an eight car formation of Class 491 stock, forming the 14.35 Waterloo to Weymouth train, and is seen descending Parkstone Bank.

Michael Collins

Plate 74 (above): Today, there is little freight traffic operated in the western extremities of the South Western Division, although a small oil terminal at Furzebrook, situated on the former Swanage branch, does bring a daily oil train, normally headed by a Class 33/1 locomotive, to the area. The train is seen here, on 20th July 1979, passing Poole Park and headed by No. 33118.

Gavin Morrison

Plate 75 (right): After the demise of steam, and prior to the commencement of the full push-pull service which ran between Bournemouth and Weymouth using modified Class 33/1 loco-motives, trains of Class 491 (TC) stock were operated by Class 33/0 machines but were unable to be controlled from the re-mote cab of the TC unit. No. D6543 emerges from Bincombe Tunnel on 18th June 1967 with a Bournemouth to Weymouth service.

John Cornelius

Plate 76 (above): The through services from Waterloo to Weymouth depart hourly from London at 00.35 minutes past each hour, these trains running fast to Southampton and then on to Bournemouth, from where the front portion goes forward to Weymouth stopping at all stations. The journey time from Waterloo to Weymouth is 2hrs. 42mins. Class 33/1 No. 33101 approaches Dorchester with the 13.35 service from Waterloo on 15th September 1979.

Gavin Morrison

Plate 77 (left): Any member of the Class 47 fleet is likely to turn up at Weymouth on a summer Saturday but, on 4th September 1982, some enthusiasts were surprised to see snowplough-fitted No. 47470 (allocated to Eastfield, Glasgow) arrive with an inter-regional service from the north. The engine is seen here at the head of the 16.00 Weymouth to Cardiff service which is formed of six Mk. I coaches and a BG.

John Vaughan

Plate 78: To gain access to Weymouth Quay, trains have to operate over the streets of the town and, during summer months, are an interest for the holiday-makers. Each day, there are two services in each direction which use the Quay Station, these being powered by Class 33/1 locomotives, on to which a special bell and flashing light is fixed giving warning of the train's approach. No. 33103 stands at the Quay Station with the 15.30 service to Waterloo on 28th March 1981.

Andrew French

SOUTHERN ROUTE
to the WEST

Plate 79 (left): Until the 1982 summer timetable came into force, when extra Waterloo to Salisbury trains, stopping at all stations en route between Basingstoke and Salisbury, were introduced, a diesel multiple unit service, formed of Class 205 stock, operated between Reading and Salisbury via Basingstoke. Arriving at Overton, on 15th April 1980, Class 205 (3H) No. 1125 forms the 09.56 Reading to Salisbury train.

Colin Marsden

Plate 80 (below): During the early 1980s, it has become regular practice to find Class 33 loco-motives with the last two digits of their number applied to the front cross plate of their bogies, thus enabling enthusiasts and photo-graphers to identify locomotives far more easily. On 7th July 1981, No. 33029 stops at Overton, with the 08.36 semi-fast train from Salisbury to Waterloo.

Colin Marsden

Plate 81 (right): The Exeter to Waterloo services usually serve all stations between Exeter and Salisbury and then run semi-fast to Waterloo, stopping only at Andover, Basingstoke and Woking and covering the 172½ miles in approximately 3hrs. 23mins. (present Type 4 schedule). Class 33 No. 33002 nears the village of Deane, near Andover, with the 07.45 Exeter to Waterloo working on a sunny 15th April 1980, probably requiring an additional five to ten minutes running time due to its lower power output.

Colin Marsden

Plate 82 (below): The crewing of Waterloo to Exeter services is maintained by drivers from only three depots. Waterloo and Salisbury men look after the Waterloo to Salisbury section while Salisbury and Exeter depots take care of the line west of Salisbury. The 17.00 service from Waterloo, in the hands of a Salisbury driver, slows for the Overton stop on 7th July 1981, with Class 50 No. 50026 *Indomitable* providing the power.

Colin Marsden

Plate 83 (above): Once a sufficient number of refurbished Class 50 locomotives became available during 1982, it was the intention of the operators to keep these modernized locomotives on the Southern route, but due to problems of diagramming, unrefurbished examples appeared on numerous services. In this view, the now refurbished No. 50050 *Fearless* pulls away from the Andover stop on 15th April 1980 with the 13.00 Waterloo to Exeter service.

Colin Marsden

Plate 87 (below right): Much of the ex-LSWR route to the west is now single line, this being reduced from double track during the 1960s in the course of economy. However, as time has come to prove, had the line been left double a much improved passenger service could have been operated with increased railway revenue. Entering the single line at Templecombe, Class 50 No. 50024 *Vanguard* heads the 14.20 Exeter to Waterloo train on 29th June 1981. This section of single track continues to Wilton Junction, a distance of twenty miles, with only one passing place, at Gillingham.

Colin Marsden

Plate 84 (above): To the east of Salisbury lies Salisbury Tunnel Junction, from where the Eastleigh and Romsey line joins the ex-LSWR main line. This cross-country connection carries a considerable amount of traffic with through services from Portsmouth to Bristol and Cardiff, along with numerous freight trains. Taking the ex-LSWR line towards Andover, Class 50 No. 50050 *Fearless* heads the 09.38 Exeter to Waterloo service on 1st July 1982.

Colin Marsden

Plate 85 (right): The old order of motive power on the West of England route was the Western Region-allocated Class 42 'Warship' locomotives. At Salisbury, in August 1971, No. D817 *Foxhound* stands next to a disused steam locomotive water-tower looking rather the worse for wear. No. D817 was still painted in maroon livery with a full yellow end when this photograph was taken.

Kevin Lane

Plate 86 (above): The refurbished Class 50 locomotives, painted in their distinctive new livery, certainly make an impressive sight when travelling through the countryside at speed. The evening light of 5th June 1982 illuminates No. 50003 *Temeraire*, photographed when setting a cracking pace on the downhill stretch through Milborne Port with the 15.10 Waterloo to Exeter train.

John Vaughan

PORTSMOUTH - BRISTOL

Plate 88 (above): Perhaps one of the few true cross-country lines in the South of England today is the Portsmouth to Bristol and Cardiff route. Since the demise of steam from these services, various types of motive power have been used, including Class 31, 33 and 35 locomotives. Today, on all but a few summer Saturday reliefs, services are operated by SR Class 33 locomotives. Awaiting to depart from Portsmouth Harbour, on 20th February 1982, Class 33 No. 33021 heads the 11.10 service to Bristol.

Colin Marsden

Plate 89 (left): Trains on this cross-country route are usually formed of five or six Mk. I coaches, providing accommodation for some 330 passengers. On 12th June 1982, the driver reopens the power controller of Class 33 No. 33018, after passing through Fratton Station at the compulsory 30m.p.h. while working the 18.10 Portsmouth Harbour to Bristol train. Part of Fratton Depot can be seen in the background.

Colin Marsden

Plate 90 (right): The Portsmouth to Bristol route diverges from the Portsmouth to Waterloo and Brighton line at Portcreek Junction, near Hilsea. From here, the line is not electrified, necessitating all trains, including the local services from Southampton to Portsmouth, to be diesel-powered. Usually these short-haul services are formed of Class 205 (3H) diesel multiple units, and No. 1131 is seen approaching Portcreek Junction with a Reading to Portsmouth, via Botley, working.

Colin Marsden

Plate 91 (left): The majority of through trains from Portsmouth to Bristol and Cardiff operate as semi-fast services after departure from Portsmouth & Southsea, stopping at Fareham, Southampton, Salisbury and thence to the Western Region. On a rather damp 12th June 1982, Class 33 No. 33003 stands at Fareham whilst working the 12.14 Bristol to Portsmouth Harbour service.

Colin Marsden

Plate 92 (right): A sight that certainly could not be repeated today is this view of Sholing Station, between Fareham and Southampton, photographed on 17th July 1959, showing two BR standard Type 2 (later Class 24) locomotives hauling the 11.35 Southampton Terminus to Fratton yard e.c.s. train. The combination had arrived at Southampton with a school special from Kent.

Richard Simmons

Plate 93 (above): The Portsmouth to Bristol journey is 103 miles in length and takes a current best timing of 2 hours 26 minutes with five intermediate stops. Carrying the well-known cross-country Portsmouth to Bristol and Cardiff headcode (89), Class 33/1 No. 33117 passes Dunbridge with the 10.10 (SO) Portsmouth Harbour to Cardiff train on 12th June 1982. It is unusual for many of the region's push-pull fitted loco-motives to be used on this route, as they are normally utilized for the Bournemouth to Weymouth, Waterloo to Salisbury (local) and, on Sundays, Reading to Portsmouth services.

Colin Marsden

Plate 94 (left): With several additional trains operating on this cross-country link on summer Saturdays, some services are diagrammed for Class 31 operation. How-ever, with a lower power output and higher locomotive weight, their performance is not on a par with the Class 33 engines. In this picture, No. 31422 nears Dean Hill, on 12th June 1982, with the 08.15 Cardiff to Portsmouth service.

Colin Marsden

Plate 95 (above): With less coaches in tow than diagrammed, Class 33 No. 33006 passes Great Wishford, on the Salisbury to Warminster section of line, with the 12.10 Portsmouth Harbour to Cardiff working on 27th November 1982. When this train arrives at Bristol, the locomotive either has to run round or another engine has to be provided for the remainder of the journey to Cardiff.

John Whiteley

Plate 96 (below): During the summer of 1981, a spur line connecting the Romsey to Salisbury and Andover to Salisbury lines was laid at a point near Salisbury Tunnel Junction, and named Laverstock Loop. Passing Laverstock South Junction, which is the loop's connection with the Romsey line, Class 33 No. 33027 *Earl Mountbatten of Burma* hauls the 10.14 Bristol to Portsmouth train on 1st August 1981.

British Railways

THE PORTSMOUTH DIRECT

Plate 97 (above): The main line between Woking and Portsmouth sees very little locomotive-hauled traffic, and throughout the week there is only one booked locomotive-hauled train to traverse the line during daylight hours, this being the 11.05 working from Portsmouth to Manchester. However, on Fridays, the 12.46 Portsmouth to Leeds train is an additional service and produces an interesting variety of motive power. The train is seen here on 30th July 1982, passing Shalford Junction, headed by Class 73s Nos. 73140 and 73113.

Andrew French

Plate 98 (left): Motive power for the 12.46 (FO) Portsmouth Harbour to Leeds service is diagrammed for a Class 33 locomotive as far as Birmingham, giving Class 33 enthusiasts a rare chance to sample an SR Type 3 deep into London Midland territory. No. 33113 passes Milford Station, on 28th January 1983, hauling a lengthy train of Mk. I stock.

Colin Marsden

Plate 99 (right): An even rarer sight on the Portsmouth direct line are the narrow-bodied Class 33/2 locomotives, normally in use on the Hastings line. No. 33208 is seen approaching Haslemere, on 25th September 1980, with the 10.56 additional empty coaching stock train from Fratton to Folkestone. The headcode carried is officially used by electric multiple unit trains operating e.c.s to Fratton from the London area!
Andrew French

Plate 100 (below): During the late 1960s, following the electrification of the Bournemouth line, a considerable amount of weekend engineering work was still necessary and Bournemouth line services were diverted via Havant and Fareham, to Eastleigh, on many occasions. As the section of line between Farlington Junction and Eastleigh was not electrified, locomotive haulage became necessary, and some interesting workings were seen on the Portsmouth line. A Birmingham RC&W Type 3, No. D6523, is pictured departing from Havant, with the 11.35 service from Weymouth to Waterloo, on 19th November 1969.
John Faulkner

Plate 101 (below): After many years of BRB policy not to name main line diesel or electric locomotives, the tables were turned during the late 1970s and early 1980s when several Class 33, 37, 47, 56, 73, 86 and 87 locomotives were allocated names. On the Southern Region, five Class 33s and four Class 73s are currently named one of which, No. 33025 *Sultan*, is pictured arriving at Portsmouth Harbour at the head of a service from Bristol during the summer of 1982.
Colin Marsden

Plate 104 (right): Some suburban branch lines of the South Western Division occasionally see locomotive-hauled trains, usually with special or excursion traffic from other regions. One such place is Windsor & Eton (Riverside) Station which, during the year, has between ten and twelve locomotive-hauled services taking passengers to see the nearby castle, the beautiful town of Windsor and the River Thames. On 17th April 1982, Class 33 locomotive No. 33016 is seen departing from Windsor & Eton (Riverside) with a return special to Nelson, Lancashire.

John Whiteley

Plate 102 (left): For many railway enthusiasts, a highlight of the modern traction era occurred on 17th October 1981, on the Southern Region, when No. 55015 *Tulyar*, a Class 55 'Deltic', visited the region on a BR sponsored railtour from the Eastern Region. Before travelling via the Portsmouth direct line to Wimbledon, Clapham Junction and back to the Eastern Region, the train visited Bournemouth, Eastleigh and Portsmouth. It is pictured at Portsmouth Harbour and displays its distinctive headboard to a large gathering of people.

Colin Marsden

Plate 103 (right): One locomotive of the Southern Region that could not be excluded from this volume is the Isle of Wight departmental shunter No. 97803. This locomotive, formerly Class 05, was shipped to the Island during the mid-1960s when steam traction was dispensed with, and electrification work was in progress. The locomotive is seen during 1982 parked at Sandown, its home for the duration of the summer. No. 97803 is only diagrammed for night permanent way duties during winter months, and on average only clocks up some fifty to eighty miles per year. It was withdrawn from service during late 1983 and was replaced by a Class 03 shunter.

Colin Marsden

Plate 105 (right): Towards the latter part of 1983, repainting of Class 73 locomotives commenced in the revised livery of wrap round yellow ends, grey roof, black window surrounds and red buffer beams, together with large BR logo and over-sized numbers. On 12th March 1984, new-liveried No. 73138 departs from Tolworth, on the Chessington branch, with the daily empty coal train bound for Acton yard and thence the South Wales coalfields.

Colin Marsden

Plate 106 (left): The Hampton Court branch, which diverges from the South Western Division main line at Hampton Court Junction, near Surbiton, does not normally see any locomotive-hauled trains. However, on 8th November 1978, the line was host to two Class 33 locomotives and a short ballast train, taken to the branch terminus in conjunction with track and platform alterations.

Colin Marsden

Plate 107 (below): Apart from operating boat trains between Waterloo, Southampton Docks and Bournemouth, the now extinct fleet of ten Class 74 electro-diesel locomotives operated a handful of London Division van and parcel trains during the later years of their lives. One of these was the 19.01 Waterloo to Staines train, seen here, on 26th July 1977, headed by No. 74001, awaiting the signal at Feltham Junction from Hounslow Junction.

Colin Marsden

Plate 108 (below): The majority of freight trains operating from the south-west, heading for the London Midland, Eastern and Western Regions or the South Eastern Division of the Southern Region normally travel via Chertsey, Staines and the Hounslow loop to either Kew Junction and the various regions, or via Clapham Junction to the South Eastern Division. Class 73 No. 73109 hauls the 09.55 Southampton 'up' yard to Halling powdered cement train, past Staines Junction on 18th September 1982, the train being formed of new privately-owned Rugby cement Presflow wagons.

Michael Collins

Plate 109 (right): To the west of Barnes Station is the junction for the Hounslow loop line from the Waterloo to Windsor and Reading line. On 13th March 1971, converging into the main line from the Hounslow loop at Barnes, the now withdrawn Class 42 No. D803 *Albion* hauls the 12.30 Exeter to Waterloo train. This service was diverted, due to engineering work, from the South Western Division main line.

John Faulkner

Plate 110 (below): One of the boundaries between the Southern and London Midland Regions exists between Latchmere Junction and Ludgate Junction (Clapham Junction). Class 33 No. 33009 is seen awaiting the signal for acceptance into Clapham Junction yard with empty stock from Liverpool (Lime Street) on 8th March 1979. The section of line between Clapham Junction and Mitre Bridge Junction is usually referred to as the West London Extension Railway (WLER).

Colin Marsden

CENTRAL DIVISION

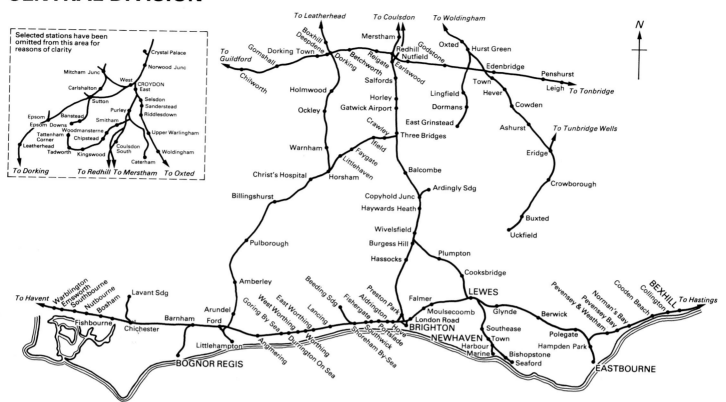

Selected stations have been omitted from this area for reasons of clarity

Plate 111: Of the three operating divisions of the Southern Region, the Central Division sees the least amount of locomotive-hauled traffic and, in fact, does not have a main line allocation of locomotives, using engines from the South Eastern and South Western Divisions' allocation. In this scene, Class 33 No. 33056 passes through Gatwick Airport Station during rebuilding work on 17th May 1980, whilst heading a train of empty coaches bound for Brighton. This locomotive and stock will form the Saturdays only service to Cardiff. However, from the introduction of the 1984 summer timetable, a new locomotive-operated 'Gatwick Express' service has been introduced using Class 73/1 locomotives and push-pull stock.

Les Bertram

Plate 112 (above): One area on the Central Division to see a considerable amount of locomotive-hauled traffic is around Norwood Junction, adjacent to Selhurst electric multiple unit depot, and situated in the maze of lines at the London side of East Croydon. To assist with route familiarization for drivers and guards, the Southern Region operates two route training saloons, these being hauled/propelled by a diesel locomotive. Here, during 1982, we see saloon No. DS70155 being propelled past Selhurst yard by Class 33 No. 33212.

Colin Marsden

Plate 113 (right): In 1937, the Southern Railway works at Ashford (Kent) produced three 0-6-0 diesel shunters, power for each locomotive being provided by an English Electric 6K engine developing 350hp. They were mainly used in the marshalling yards at Norwood, where No. S1 was photographed during early 1940. After nationalization this locomotive became No. 15201. The two downward sloping windows in the cab back bulkhead give the crew a clear view of the coupling and vacuum-pipe during shunting movements.

GEC Traction Ltd.

Plate 114 (above): During the late 1950s and 1960s several excursion trains from the Midland and Eastern regions to the South Coast were formed of diesel multiple unit stock, thus removing both the necessity for running round trains at their destinations and the provision of locomotive servicing facilities. An eight car formation, led by a Metro-Cammell twin set approaches South Croydon on 17th May 1964 with a holiday preview special from Walsall to Brighton.

John Scrace

Plate 115 (below): Passing the now redundant main line platforms at Coulsdon North, on 19th October 1982, is push-pull fitted Class 33/1 No. 33118, in charge of the 09.35 Salfords Oil Terminal to Stanlow (LMR) empty aviation fuel tank train. It is very unusual to see South Western Division-allocated Class 33/1 locomotives operating away from their native division.

Colin Marsden

Plate 116 (above): At Coulsdon North, the Central Division main line splits into two sections, the fast lines continuing via the Quarry line to Earlswood, and the local tracks running via Redhill. Traversing the 'down' local line, and about to take the points for Coulsdon South, Merstham and Redhill stations on 19th October 1982, is Class 73/0 No. 73002 hauling special empties from New Cross Gate to Eastbourne. *Colin Marsden*

Plate 117 (right): Until January 1983, stone for permanent way workings arrived on the Central Division from quarries on the Western Region via Woking, Guildford and the cross-country line through Reigate. However, from January 1983, it was decided to divert all Central and South Eastern Division stone trains via the coast route from Westbury, by way of Fareham, Havant and the coastway line to Chichester. Class 33/1 locomotive No. 33102 arrives at Redhill yard with the 08.20 Woking to Three Bridges working on 28th April 1982. *Colin Marsden*

Plate 118 (left): A daily freight train that traverses the Central Division main line by way of Redhill is the 09.06 Salfords to Cliffe empty aggregate train, formed of nine privately-owned high capacity bogie hoppers. On 28th April 1982, the train was headed by Class 73/1 No. 73103, passing the soon to be redundant Redhill signal box. This train normally travels via East Croydon, Clapham Junction and Factory Junction to the South Eastern Division.

Colin Marsden

Plate 119 (below): Earlswood, to the south of Redhill, is where the Quarry line and the Redhill line rejoin with a considerable number of crossovers provided, enabling fast and slow trains to be transferred. An electric multiple unit formation is seen traversing the 'up' Quarry line. Taking the 'down' local line from Redhill is Class 33/1 locomotive No. 33102 heading a stone train formed of 'Dace' wagons en route to Three Bridges.

Colin Marsden

Plate 120 (right): Throughout the duration of the 1982/3 timetable, a maximum of seventeen freight trains in each direction were booked to pass Earlswood during a 24 hour period, the majority of these being either dated or operated by night, and the photographer has difficulty in finding a locomotive-hauled subject to capture. Class 73 No. 73123 passes Earlswood, on 9th March 1982, with the 09.06 Salfords to Cliffe train.

Colin Marsden

Plate 121 (below): Twenty six members of the Class 33 fleet are fitted with miniature snowploughs and, during periods of inclement weather, are stabled at strategic locations where heavy snow may necessitate ploughing. However, snowploughs fitted to locomotives are only intended for shallow drifts, and anything more than about 15in. requires the use of a larger converted steam locomotive tender plough. Class 33 No. 33004, carrying miniature snowploughs, is seen passing Three Bridges, on 22nd February 1982, with an oil train heading south.

Colin Marsden

VSOE on the CENTRAL

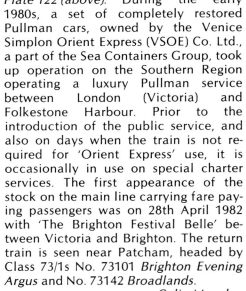

Plate 122 (above): During the early 1980s, a set of completely restored Pullman cars, owned by the Venice Simplon Orient Express (VSOE) Co. Ltd., a part of the Sea Containers Group, took up operation on the Southern Region operating a luxury Pullman service between London (Victoria) and Folkestone Harbour. Prior to the introduction of the public service, and also on days when the train is not required for 'Orient Express' use, it is occasionally in use on special charter services. The first appearance of the stock on the main line carrying fare paying passengers was on 28th April 1982 with 'The Brighton Festival Belle' between Victoria and Brighton. The return train is seen near Patcham, headed by Class 73/1s No. 73101 *Brighton Evening Argus* and No. 73142 *Broadlands*.

Colin Marsden

Plate 123 (left): Much interest was taken in the train once it commenced operation and, for several weeks, the arrivals and departures from Victoria were recorded by the world's press. On 17th August 1982, the British Broadcasting Corporation (BBC) hired the train for filming purposes when it operated between Victoria and Bognor Regis, via Horsham, powered by Class 73/1 No. 73142 *Broadlands*, seen in this illustration approaching Horsham.

John Scrace

Plate 124 (above): Nearing the southern extremity of the Mid-Sussex line at Arundel, the BBC special from Victoria to Bognor Regis is seen headed by Class 73/1 No. 73142 *Broadlands*. The VSOE train, when in passenger service, is normally formed of seven Pullman vehicles and a baggage van. Whilst the BBC film team were at work at Bognor Regis, one of the platforms took on the identity of Folkestone Harbour!

John Vaughan

Plate 125 (right): The 'Orient Express' Pullman coaches were chartered by a party of race-goers, on 5th September 1982. A Class 73/1 locomotive, No. 73122, was diagrammed to work the train from London (Victoria) to Arundel, where passengers left the train to be conveyed by road to Goodwood Racecourse. The special then continued to Littlehampton to run round and berth. The locomotive is seen here being attached to the stock in the yard at Littlehampton, watched by various members of the operating CM&EE department and train crew members.

John Vaughan

Plate 126 (above): The area around Horsham is in the heart of electric multiple unit country but, with a sizeable power supply and privately-owned fertilizer sidings nearby, a number of locomotive-hauled movements do occur. One through service which operated for several years via the Mid-Sussex line to Horsham, and thence via Three Bridges to gain the Central Division main line, was the daily Eastleigh to Norwood freight train, normally powered by an electro-diesel locomotive. On 16th May 1973, the train is seen near Ifield headed by No. E6016.   *John Scrace*

Plate 127 (below): With a mixture of carflats, ferryvans and box vans in tow, one of the six prototype electro-diesels of Type JA, No. E6002, nears Horsham with the Norwood to Eastleigh freight working on 4th March 1973. The first six electro-diesels are immediately recognizable from the remainder of the fleet by having an additional jumper cable under the driving cab window.   *John Scrace*

Plate 128 (right): A superb period photograph of Horsham, taken on 19th July 1959, which shows a four car formation of original Metro-Cammell lightweight diesel multiple unit stock approaching the station with an excursion from Southend (Central), is seen passing the SR-designed signal box and large yards. In the background, waiting in the sidings, is Class M7 0-4-4T No. 30132 with the stock for the 12.38 Horsham to Guildford, via Christ's Hospital, service.

John Scrace

Plate 129 (below): Although Horsham Station is on the Central Division, it is served by passenger trains of both the Central and South Western Divisions. One train firmly in the hands of Central Division's operating powers is this Class 73-hauled ballast train, standing in Horsham 'up' Central Division platform, with 350 tons of new track ballast for renewal work at the nearby Horsham Junction. The scene was photographed on 18th April 1982, and the locomotive pictured is No. 73124.

Bill Walker

. . . and DOWN the MID SUSSEX

Plate 130 (right): Rare power appeared on the Mid-Sussex line on 26th March 1978 when the 'Deltic'-hauled DAA Railtour Society's 'The Man of Kent' tour from London Bridge, which had the majority of its itinerary in Sussex, traversed the line. It was photographed while departing from the short Amberley Tunnel, south of Amberley Station, headed by No. 55007 *Pinza*, whilst en route for Littlehampton and Bognor Regis.

John Vaughan

Plate 132 (above):   A truly local freight train, which has survived into the 1980s, is the 08.50 Brighton to Fratton and the 12.45 return service. On 19th August 1982, the motive power provided by Brighton Depot was Class 73/1 No. 73120, this locomotive having a soft job as it passed Goring-by-Sea with only five coal wagons and a ferry van in tow.

John Vaughan

Plate 133 (below):   Today the Southern Region is a 'fully-fitted' region, meaning that all trains must have a continuous brake throughout all vehicles, unless special authorization is given by the traffic control office. Class 73/1 No. 73123 has forty vacuum-braked coal wagons in harness as it leaves West Worthing and heads for the coal distribution depot at Hove, with the 12.45 Fratton to Brighton freight on 23rd August 1982.

John Vaughan

Plate 131 (left):   The coastway route from Ore to Portsmouth sees few locomotive-hauled trains, apart from trip and ballast workings. However, a main line locomotive-hauled passenger train visited the line on 30th August 1982 when Class 47/3 No. 47373, complete with flashing roof light, hauled an Alfreton & Mansfield Parkway to Bognor Regis excursion, seen here between Worthing and Durrington stations. Passengers on board were able to spend some 4½ hours at the Sussex resort before returning home.

John Vaughan

THE READING - TONBRIDGE CONNECTION

Plate 134 (above): The Reading to Tonbridge cross-country connection, which is operated by diesel electric multiple unit and diesel multiple unit stock, is one of the most useful non-arterial routes of the Southern Region, giving a connection between the Western Region and the South Western, Central and South Eastern Divisions. Starting out on its 65¾ mile journey from Reading to Tonbridge is a Western Region-allocated Class 119 diesel multiple unit carrying the number L592. It is seen, in late summer 1982, approaching Reading Spur Junction.

Colin Marsden

Plate 135 (below): A new service introduced during the early 1980s provided trains from Reading to Gatwick Airport, via Guildford and Redhill. These trains operate fast over the Reading to Redhill section and provide an efficient link for passengers travelling on the Western Region whose destination is Gatwick Airport. Class 119 set No. L575, with Gatwick Airport on the indicator, approaches Wanborough on a sunny 13th May 1982.

Colin Marsden

Plate 136 (right): Prior to the introduction of Western Region diesel multiple unit stock on the route, trains were operated by the unique 3R 'Tadpole' units, introduced during the 1960s. These 3R sets were formed by disbanding various 6S units and remarshalling the vehicles with EPB electric multiple unit driving trailer vehicles, giving a 'Tadpole' appearance of one wide and two narrow bodied vehicles within one unit. Set No. 1205 is pictured arriving at Shalford during 1979.

Colin Marsden

Plate 137 (below): The last 'Tadpole' unit was withdrawn during 1983 but, prior to this, it was often kept spare at St. Leonards Depot. Set No. 1206, with MBSO leading, approaches the staggered platforms at Gomshall, on 3rd May 1979, with a Reading to Tonbridge train. During 1980, set No. 1206 was reformed with vehicles from former 6L units.

John Vaughan

Plate 138 (left): Although the journey between Reading and Tonbridge is only 65¾ miles, the average time taken is 2hrs. 31mins., with 24 intermediate stops. Passing through the Surrey countryside, near Deepdene, is the 14.51 Tonbridge to Reading working of 17th April 1982. These three car Western Region diesel multiple units can accommodate 18 first class and 144 second class passengers, whereas the former Class 206 (3R) units could only accommodate 140 second class passengers.

Colin Marsden

Plate 139 (below): During the mid-1970s, locomotive-hauled formations of three or four vehicles operated the Reading to Redhill section of the cross-country link during peak periods, providing additional services to the hourly diesel multiple units. Class 33 locomotive No. 33004 stands at Redhill at the head of the 16.40 to Reading on 17th July 1975.

Brian Morrison

Plate 140 (right): Crossing the Surrey/Kent boundary near Edenbridge, Class 119 set No. L574 forms the 10.16 Reading to Tonbridge train on 28th April 1982. Class 119 units were modified internally for use on the Reading to Tonbridge line with passenger luggage storage areas being provided in the DMBC and TS vehicles, these areas being labelled on both the outside and inside of each vehicle.

Colin Marsden

Plate 141 (below): One cross-country service that used the Tonbridge to Reading connection for many years were the Margate to Birkenhead holiday trains. During the late 1950s and early 1960s these were frequently powered by BR standard Type 2 (later Class 24) locomotives, being used at that time on the Southern Region, whilst delays were being experienced in delivery of their Birmingham RC&W Type 3 locomotives. Type 2 No. D5002 passes over the Edenbridge town line, near Edenbridge, with the 'up' country working during July 1960.

Derek Cross

BRANCH LINES

Plate 142 (left): Central Division operate two branch or secondary routes that are worked by diesel traction, these being the line between London and Uckfield and the branch to East Grinstead from Hurst Green. Also working on to the line at Eridge is the branch from Tunbridge Wells West. Seen here in the bay platform at Eridge on 10th August 1982, is a Tunbridge Wells train formed of Class 207 (3D) unit No. 1319.

Colin Marsden

Plate 143 (below): Hourly services operate on the Uckfield line except during peak periods. Services are normally operated from London (Victoria) but during the early 1980s, due to engineering work, services have been operating from London Bridge. Trains from London are normally formed of six cars as far as Oxted, from where one portion goes to East Grinstead and the other to Uckfield. Class 207 No. 1303 is seen departing from Crowborough in this August 1982 view.

Colin Marsden

Plate 144 (above): The hourly shuttle between Eridge and Tunbridge Wells has to be formed of Class 207 units, as the tunnel clearances on the route do not permit the use of standard width vehicles of Class 205. Arriving at Tunbridge Wells West on 3rd July 1981 is Class 207 No. 1311. It is intended to close this line in the foreseeable future.

John Glover

Plate 145 (right): During peak periods, some services on both the London Bridge to Uckfield and East Grinstead routes are operated by locomotive-hauled formations, which is mainly due to insufficient diesel electric multiple units being available. However, this situation is likely to change within a few years, when the remaining handful of locomotive-hauled commuter services will disappear. On 10th August 1982, Class 33 No. 33014 passes Cowden with the 17.20 London Bridge to Uckfield service.

Colin Marsden

SOUTH EASTERN DIVISION

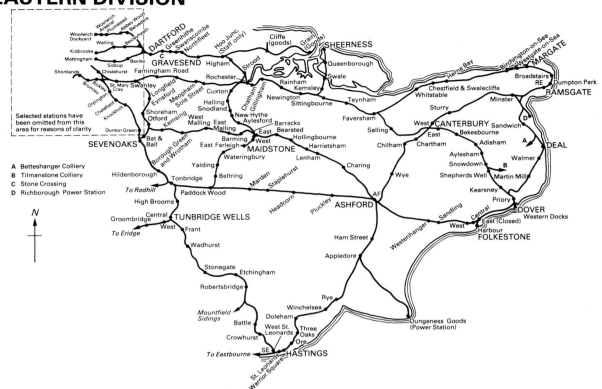

A Betteshanger Colliery
B Tilmanstone Colliery
C Stone Crossing
D Richborough Power Station

Selected stations have been omitted from this area for reasons of clarity

N

Plate 146: One of the first inroads into steam superiority on the South Eastern Division came during the late 1950s when, due to prolonged delivery of the SR's Birmingham RC&W Type 3 locomotives, the region was loaned a number of BR standard Type 2 locomotives. These intruders were allocated to the South Eastern Division and could be found operating many main line passenger duties in addition to numerous freight trains. No. D5010 traverses the Chislehurst Loop at St. Mary Cray with an unfitted freight train during May 1959.

Derek Cross

BICKLEY JUNCTION

Plate 147 (above): To the south of Bromley are the sizeable junctions of Bickley and St. Mary Cray, and it is here that the main line from Hither Green to Sevenoaks is crossed by the main London to North Kent route. With a total of 3,200hp available, two Class 73/1s, Nos. 73107 and 73117, haul the daily Betteshanger Colliery to Tyne Yard merry-go-round train under the Sevenoaks to Hither Green line, and past Bickley Junction.
Colin Marsden

Plate 148 (right): For several years after the demise of steam traction, a train that brought interesting motive power to the tracks of the South Eastern Division was the daily coal train from the London Midland Region to Gravesend, usually formed of 16 ton four-wheeled coal wagons and frequently hauled by a Class 45 'Peak' locomotive. On 28th August 1974, No. 45130 approaches Chislehurst Junction from Bickley Junction with the southbound working.
Brian Morrison

Plate 149 (left): Between the demise of steam traction and the full introduction of the Kent Coast electrification scheme, the South Eastern Division main line to Ramsgate, Margate and Dover was operated by diesel locomotives. No. D6505, a Birmingham RC&W Type 3, was only three months old, when photographed with a London to Dover boat train, during July 1960, passing Chelsfield. Of particular interest are the steam style identification discs fixed to the front lamp irons.

Derek Cross

Plate 150 (below): Today the main diesel power on the London to Tonbridge route is the hourly diesel electric multiple unit formations operating the Charing Cross/Cannon Street to Hastings trains. Units of three types operate this service; 6S (six car short frame), 5L and 6L (five or six car long frame) vehicles. In this view of Hildenborough Bank, taken on 12th May 1973, 6S set No. 1006 forms a Charing Cross to Hastings service.

Brian Morrison

ONWARDS to TONBRIDGE

Plate 151 (above): Carrying headcode 4, which indicates that the train is travelling between Charing Cross and Margate, via Orpington and Dover, Birmingham RC&W Type 3 No. D6503 approaches Tonbridge on 6th June 1960, only three months after delivery from its builders in Smethwick. When delivered, the Birmingham RC&W Type 3 engines were the first purpose-built e.t.h.-fitted locomotives in service, and problems arose when insufficient electrically-heated stock was available. Initially, therefore, BR Type 2 locomotives, fitted with steam heating, were coupled between the SR locomotive and passenger trains to provide a heating supply.

Author's Collection

Plate 152 (below): A source of freight traffic and therefore revenue to the South Eastern Division are the docks situated at Dover, with numerous perishable goods trains, conveying European produce, daily traversing the tracks to all corners of the country. On 16th August 1960, Birmingham RC&W Type 3 No. D6510 passes Tonbridge with an 'up' working bound for the London Midland Region.

John Scrace

DEMUs TOWARDS HASTINGS

Plate 153 (left): The line from Tonbridge to Hastings was not electrified as part of the Kent Coast electrification scheme of the late 1950s, and with restricted clearances on the route necessitating stock to be no wider than 9ft. 0in., the choice of new stock for the line was limited. The first of the purpose-built Hastings line diesel electric multiple unit sets emerged during 1957, and have been in operation ever since. A 6L set, No. 1012, passes High Brooms, between Tonbridge and Tunbridge Wells, on 10th August 1982, with a Hastings to Charing Cross train.

Colin Marsden

Plate 154 (right): When introduced, the six car Hastings diesel electric multiple unit stock was painted in distinctive SR green livery. However, progression has taken over and the sets now carry standard Inter-City colours of blue and grey, with smaller numerals. In its original condition, 6L set No. 1018 is shown near Grove Junction with the 13.20 Charing Cross to Hastings working on 24th May 1958.

John Scrace

Plate 155 (left): The distinctive former ex-LBSCR station buildings at Tunbridge Wells West, which opened their doors to passengers in 1866 (although much of the building was rebuilt during 1906), forms the backdrop to this view of Class 207 (3D) No. 1301, forming the 16.34 Eridge to Tonbridge train of 6th May 1980. On the left, in the background, is the stabling point housing another 3D unit.

Brian Morrison

Plate 156 (right): The station at Stonegate, situated deep in the heart of the Kent countryside and 43¾ miles from London, has staggered platforms and only receives an infrequent service during off-peak periods. On 10th August 1982, a 6L set, No. 1012, forming the 13.45 Charing Cross to Hastings service, is seen passing the 'up' platform with its ex-SECR wooden waiting shelter.
Colin Marsden

Plate 157 (left): The area around Hastings is a mass of tunnels, with the stations of St. Leonards, (Warrior Square) and Hastings situated between. Emerging from Hastings Tunnel and approaching Hastings Station is an immaculate 6L set No. 1014, forming the 17.36 Cannon Street to Hastings train. This service runs fast to Tonbridge, then on to Tunbridge Wells where it is split, the front portion running fast from there to Robertsbridge and then all stations to Hastings, whilst the rear portion runs semi-fast omitting Robertsbridge, Battle and Crowhurst. *Colin Marsden*

Plate 158 (below): The allocation of the Hastings diesel electric multiple unit fleet is centred on West St. Leonards Depot, situated some three quarters of a mile to the west of West St. Leonards Station on the coastway line. The depot has an allocation of 57 units made up of 232 cars. In this Sunday morning view of the depot no less than six of the Hastings main line units can be seen. *Andrew French*

Plate 159 (above): A pleasant branch line of the 1980s is the 26½ mile stretch of line between Hastings and Ashford. Once part of the main arterial network of the South Eastern Railway, it is now a single track except for the section between Ashford and Appledore. Passing the now residential station buildings at Winchelsea, 3D set No. 1308 approaches the somewhat desolate platform with the 17.27 Hastings to Ashford working of 27th July 1982.

Colin Marsden

Plate 160 (below): The last surviving member of the 'Tadpole' fleet, No. 1206, was often used on Ashford to Hastings duties, and was observed on 27th July 1982 approaching Ham Street with the 15.47 Hastings to Ashford train. Passenger services on the line are hourly, with few additional services during the peak period. The 26½ mile journey takes fifty minutes, with seven intermediate stops.

Colin Marsden

Plate 161 (right): A continuous parade of electric multiple units is usually seen on the South Eastern Division's main line through Tonbridge to Ashford and Folkestone to the Kent coast, although several daily locomotive-hauled freight trains, and more recently the three times weekly VSOE Pullman locomotive-hauled services, do traverse the line. On 4th April 1979, Class 33/0 No. 33061 was captured on film near Marden with a southbound coal and freight train from Norwood to Ashford.

Colin Marsden

Plate 162 (below): For the conveyance of perishable produce between Dover docks and the fruit terminal at Paddock Wood, a daily transfer freight operates, departing from Dover at 10.20 and returning from Paddock Wood at 12.30. The train is usually formed of privately-owned Continental rolling stock, and is seen here passing the hop fields near Paddock Wood, on 4th June 1982, with the 'up' service, headed by Class 33/0 No. 33047.

Colin Marsden

Plate 163: A train that could hardly have been economic to operate was this Hither Green to Ashford fitted freight working, formed of only one bogie bolster wagon loaded with sleepers. The train was observed on the outskirts of Ashford on 15th May 1980 headed by Class 33/0 No. 33050. The locomotive hauling this train is always recognizable from the rest of the fleet, because of a cut-out just above the coupling on the front end.

Colin Marsden

Plate 164 (above): Between Sandling and Folkestone are the loops of Cheriton. Seen traversing the 'up' relief line is the daily vans train from Margate to New Cross Gate headed by one of the Southern Region's four named Class 73s, No. 73101 *Brighton Evening Argus*, and photographed on 3rd June 1982. When this engine was named on 3rd December 1980 it was temporarily renumbered 73100. *Colin Marsden*

Plate 165 (left): With a superb collection of pre-nationalization stock in tow, BR Type 2 No. D5010 passes near Sandling Junction, once the junction for the Hythe and Sandgate branch, with an 'up' country vans train during the summer of 1960. Soon after this photograph was taken, a number of Type 2 locomotives working on the Southern Region were taken out of service as their axle loading was found to be in excess of the laid down maximum. However, this was overcome by the removal of train heating equipment and boiler water tanks. *Derek Cross*

Plate 166 (left): The VSOE Pullman service, between London and Venice, operates twice a week in each direction but, due to an inbalance of movements, the train is actually used on three days. This involves running from Folkestone to Victoria on Thursdays, from Victoria to Folkestone on Fridays, and on Sundays a return trip is operated. For movement between Folkestone (East) and Folkestone Harbour, the train is operated with a locomotive at both ends, as restricted runround facilities exist at the harbour station. On 3rd June 1982, No. 73124 hauls the stock towards the harbour with No. 73142 *Broadlands* at the rear. *Colin Marsden*

Plate 167 (above):   With the little signal cabin of Folkestone Warren behind the fourth vehicle, Birmingham RC&W Type 3 No. D6532 hauls an unfitted freight train towards Folkestone from the Dover direction on 12th June 1961. The coastway section of line between Dover and Folkestone is often subjected to landslides and rock falls, and to prevent any possible danger to trains, a 'tripwire' system has been installed which indicates to the signalman when such a fall has taken place.

Derek Cross

Plate 168 (below):   A period view of Margate Station, taken on 28th April 1961, when steam traction still reigned supreme on the South Eastern main line. In the sidings behind BR Type 2 No. D5013, no less than six steam locomotives can be seen. Margate Station was first opened in 1863 but the present station, seen here, was reconstructed in 1926. Note the interesting water-towers in the yard and on the platform ends.

British Railways

AROUND FAVERSHAM

Plate 169 (above): Faversham, on the North Kent route to the south, is the junction where the line to Dover, via Margate, diverges from the Dover, via Canterbury, route. With the now closed motive power depot in the background, Class 73/1 No. 73114 passes the signal box and electric multiple unit stabling point, with a Dover to Bescot perishable goods train on Sunday, 26th September 1982.
Colin Marsden

Plate 170 (right): Pulling out of Faversham Station and taking the Margate line, Class 73/1 No. 73114 hauls the 14.03 Hoo Junction to Herne Bay ballast train, formed of ten high-capacity 'Sealion' hoppers. Parked in the stabling point another Class 73/1 locomotive, No. 73140 can be seen. All the tracks to the right of this picture were once electrified by the SR's 750 volts d.c. overhead system, as fitted to the now extinct Class 71 straight electric locomotives.
Colin Marsden

SHEERNESS FREIGHT

Plate 171 (above): A South Eastern branch line which can provide some interesting movements is the one to Sheerness, which diverges from the main line at Sittingbourne. The various private sidings at Ridham, Queenborough and Sheerness are host to several trains each day. Approaching Queenborough with a train of scrap bound for Sheerness Steelworks is Class 73/1 No. 73104, pictured on 26th August 1981.

Brian Morrison

Plate 172 (below): The Sheerness branch has double track as far as Swale, from where it is single throughout to Sheerness, with a passing place at Queenborough. Carrying an appropriate headcode, (ED), Class 73/1 No. 73107 hauls a lengthy empty coal train, with a bogie bolster on the rear, towards Kingsferry with the 11.25 Sheerness to Ridham trip freight of 27th July 1982.

Colin Marsden

LONDON via the SECR ROUTE

Plate 173 (above): A sight to make most enthusiasts of Class 33s go weak at the knees, is this view of Nos. 33029 and 33009 hauling loaded merry-go-round wagons from Betteshanger Colliery, bound for the London Midland Region and viewed over the rooftops near Chatham on 29th May 1981. With the two Class 33 locomotives working in multiple, the driver has 3,100hp available to haul the 1,000 + ton train.
Colin Marsden

Plate 174 (right): Prior to the introduction of Class 56s on the Northfleet-bound merry-go-round coal trains from the Midland and Derbyshire pits, the trains were entrusted to pairs of London Midland Region Type 4s of either Class 45 or 47, and on numerous occasions mixed pairs were recorded. This view, taken inside the Northfleet cement works, shows a Class 47 locomotive, No. 47201, in tandem with Class 45 No. 45043 *The King's Own Royal Border Regiment*, passing through the discharge hoppers.
Michael Collins

Plate 176 (above): With Northfleet Station in the background, and the entrance to the cement works on the left, Class 73/1 No. 73124 hauls a train of only six HTV wagons bound for Hoo Junction. The train only slightly outweighs the locomotive and therefore the 1,600hp available from the locomotive, operating under electric conditions, should be adequate to shift the load.

Colin Marsden

Plate 177 (right): Over recent years, it has become an increasingly common practice for Southern Region drivers to use two white blanks as the headcode of their train, instead of finding out and displaying the correct code for the type of train and route to be covered. Class 73 No. 73124 is seen passing Greenhithe with a southbound ABS train formed of five modern high capacity four wheel vehicles on 29th May 1981.

Colin Marsden

Plate 175 (left): One of the base ingredients used in the manufacture of cement is gypsum, which is transported to the Northfleet works by train from the British Gypsum terminal at Mountfield, near Battle. The train normally operates daily, and is formed of a scaled-down version of the standard MGR wagon, purpose-built for its charge. Hastings gauge Class 33/2 No. 33205 is seen arriving at Northfleet on one of these trains on 29th May 1981.

Colin Marsden

Plate 178 (left): A distinctive landmark at Dartford for the railway photographer is the sub-station and powerhouse, situated in the junction between the Dartford Loop line and the route from the Mid and North Kent lines. Approaching Dartford from the Dartford Loop, on 26th October 1982, is Class 73/0 electro-diesel No. 73003, hauling the 13.10 Stewarts Lane stone terminal to Cliffe empty stone hopper train.

Michael Collins

Plate 179 (below): Any Southern Region main line locomotives of either Class 33 or 73 requiring heavy body repairs are usually dealt with at the CM&EE repair shops at Slade Green, situated on the North Kent line, near Dartford. Over recent years the repair shop has had several major collision repairs to undertake, including the complete rebuilding of one end of No. 33056 *The Burma Star.* In this illustration, taken during February 1982, No. 33064 is seen under repair after receiving serious frontal collision damage.

Plate 180 (right): During the summer months, the majority of snowplough-fitted Class 33 locomotives have their centre plough removed, following complaints from Western Region shunting staff who experienced difficulties with uncoupling and coupling locomotives so fitted to and from coaches. 'Slim Jim' Class 33/2 No. 33212, complete with snowploughs, passes Crayford on the Dartford Loop with a train of oil tanks on 23rd April 1982.

Andrew French

Plate 181 (below): Of the three routes to Dartford from the London Division, the majority of non-passenger trains operate on the Dartford Loop line via Sidcup, and on most days a wide variety of locomotive classes and train types can be recorded. With a cartic-4, an oil tank and a gypsum hopper in tow, Class 33/0 No. 33054 travels between Crayford and Bexley with a Hoo Junction bound freight train on 29th May 1981.

Colin Marsden

Plate 182 (above): From 1979, the purpose-built Class 56 freight locomotives started operating on to Southern Region tracks with daily merry-go-round trains from pits in the Midlands and Derbyshire to the Northfleet cement works. Prior to their introduction, trains were shorter in length and double-headed by two Type 4 locomotives. With 36 empty hoppers in tow, Class 56 No. 56058 grinds away near Bexley with the 12.56 Northfleet to Toton empties working of 17th January 1980.

Brian Morrison

Plate 183 (left): New Eltham Station is pictured in the background, as the 09.02 aggregate train from Cliffe (Brett Marine stone terminal), to Stewarts Lane cement terminal, on 5th May 1982, is headed by Class 33 No. 33065. After arriving at Stewarts Lane, the locomotive is detached and 'stood off' whilst the train is unloaded, and about 13.00 is reattached to depart at 13.10 with the empty hoppers for Cliffe.

Colin Marsden

KENT's SECONDARY ROUTES

Plate 184 (above): Some of the secondary routes in Kent, and in particular those in and around Maidstone, have some interesting locomotive-hauled trains. Each day a Class 73 takes an oil train from Hoo Junction to Brookgate Oil Terminal, near Aylesford, but as the entrance to the terminal is on the 'up' line, the train travels to Maidstone West to run round. On 4th June 1982, Class 73 No. 73123 is pictured passing Aylesford whilst en route to Maidstone West.
Colin Marsden

Plate 185 (right): It is impossible to get a train any shorter than this! The 08.40 Hoo Junction to Woking CCE train, formed of just one vehicle, is headed by a Class 33/0 locomotive, No. 33064 and was photographed as it approached Maidstone Barracks Station, about to pass under the Maidstone East line on 3rd June 1982. The vehicle behind the engine is a 'Dace' stone wagon, conforming to T.O.P.S. code ZDV.
Colin Marsden

Plate 186 (left): With catenary poles still surviving from the overhead electrification in Tovil yard, Maidstone, Class 33/0 No. 33046 hauls the daily 18.20 Hoo Junction to Salfords oil train on 3rd June 1982. This train runs via Tonbridge and Redhill where it runs round, arriving at its destination at 21.44. It is interesting to note that one bogie tanker has been marshalled in the formation of short wheelbase vehicles.
Colin Marsden

Plate 187 (right): The cross-country connection between the North Kent routes at Strood, and the Mid-Kent line at Paddock Wood, provides a useful link for freight services. However, in recent years with the general decline in freight traffic, fewer trains now use the line. Type JB electro-diesel No. E6036, painted in early blue livery with small yellow warning panel, passes the beautiful little country station of Wateringbury at the head of a coal train on 14th August 1970.
John Scrace

Plate 188 (below): The section of line between Swanley and Ashford, via Maidstone, sees little locomotive-hauled activity, with most freight traffic running via Tonbridge. The pioneer electro-diesel, No. E6001, still sporting oval buffers, is seen passing Eynsford Station with a southbound Continental ferry train on 28th August 1970 and, at this time, the station still had green enamel signs.
John Scrace